IT'S MOTHERFUCKING PLEASURE

by Sam Brewer, Aarian Mehrabani
Chloe Palmer & Josh Roche

Based on an original concept
by Samuel Brewer

ISBN 978-0-573-00036-2

concordtheatricals.co.uk
concordtheatricals.com

FOR AMATEUR PRODUCTION ENQUIRIES

UNITED KINGDOM AND WORLD
EXCLUDING NORTH AMERICA
licensing@concordtheatricals.co.uk

020-7054-7298

Each title is subject to availability from Concord Theatricals, depending upon country of performance.

This work is published by Samuel French, an imprint of Concord Theatricals Ltd.

The Professional Rights in this play are controlled by Concord Theatricals Ltd, Aldwych House, 71-91 Aldwych, London, WC2B 4HN.

scanned, uploaded, or transmitted in any form, by any means, now known or yet to be invented, including mechanical, electronic, digital, photocopying, recording, videotaping, or otherwise, without the prior written permission of the publisher. No one shall share this title, or part of this title, to any social media or file hosting websites.

The moral right of Sam Brewer, Aarian Mehrabani, Chloe Palmer & Josh Roche (FlawBored) to be identified as author of this work has been asserted in accordance with Section 77 of the Copyright, Designs and Patents Act 1988.

USE OF COPYRIGHTED MUSIC

A licence issued by Concord Theatricals to perform this play does not include permission to use the incidental music specified in this publication. In the United Kingdom: Where the place of performance is already licensed by the PERFORMING RIGHT SOCIETY (PRS) a return of the music used must be made to them. If the place of performance is not so licensed then application should be made to PRS for Music (www.prsformusic.com). A separate and additional licence from PHONOGRAPHIC PERFORMANCE LTD (www.ppluk.com) may be needed whenever commercial recordings are used. Outside the United Kingdom: Please contact the appropriate music licensing authority in your territory for the rights to any incidental music.

USE OF COPYRIGHTED THIRD-PARTY MATERIALS

Licensees are solely responsible for obtaining formal written permission from copyright owners to use copyrighted third-party materials (e.g., artworks, logos) in the performance of this play and are strongly cautioned to do so. If no such permission is obtained by the licensee, then the licensee must use only original materials that the licensee owns and controls. Licensees are solely responsible and liable for clearances of all third-party copyrighted materials, and shall indemnify the copyright owners of the play(s) and their licensing agent, Concord Theatricals Ltd., against any costs, expenses, losses and liabilities arising from the use of such copyrighted third-party materials by licensees.

IMPORTANT BILLING AND CREDIT REQUIREMENTS

If you have obtained performance rights to this title, please refer to your licensing agreement for important billing and credit requirements.

IT'S A MOTHERF**KING PLEASURE was first produced by FlawBored and ASYLUM Arts at Vaults Festival February 2023. The cast was as follows:

SAM / TIM .... Samuel Brewer
CHLOE / HELEN RICHARDSON .... Chloe Palmer
AARIAN / ROSS .... Aarian Mehrabani

CREATIVE TEAM

Writers | Sam Brewer, Aarian Mehrabani, Chloe Palmer & Josh Roche
Director | Josh Roche
Producer | Stephen Bailey for ASYLUM Arts
Designer | Cara Evans
Associate Designer | Ana Webb-Sanchez
Lighting Designers | Alex Musgrave and Abi Turner
Sound Designer | Calum Perrin
Video Designer | Dan Light
Associate Video Designer | Josie Ireland
Production Stage Manager |Beatrice Galloway
Stage Manager | Lauren Hastings
Access Worker | Victoria Hoyle

IT'S A MOTHERF**KING PLEASURE then transferred to Soho Theatre in May 2023. The stage manager was Beatrice Galloway, it was produced by ASYLUM Arts with Hannah Smith and the lighting designer was Alex Musgrave.

IT'S A MOTHERF**KING PLEASURE will transfer to the Edinburgh Festival with support from New Diorama Theatre and Underbelly, as one of the winners of the Untapped Award 2023.

FlawBored

FlawBored is a multi-award winning disabled-led theatre company.
Co-founded by Samuel Brewer, Aarian Mehrabani and Chloe Palmer.
It's A Motherf**king Pleasure is their debut show and aims to address
complex and uncomfortable issues surrounding identity – which no one
has the answers to. FlawBored strives to make work that is challenging,
funny and accessible.

CAST

SAMUEL BREWER | SAM / TIM

Samuel Brewer is one of the co-founders of FlawBored and co-writer of *It's A Motherf**king Pleasure.*

Samuel trained on the BA Acting Collaborative and Devised Theatre course at the Royal Central School of Speech and Drama, graduating in 2020.

Since graduating he has worked as an actor, voice-over artist, theatremaker, educator and access consultant. Working as a visiting professional for the Royal Central School of Speech and Drama, East 15 and Guildhall. Working with companies such as: The Watermill Theatre, Shakespeare's Globe, Complicité, Pentabus Theatre, Leeds Playhouse, and ASYLUM Arts (who he frequently collaborates with). He works frequently as an access consultant and audio description consultant. Samuel will often find himself working with playwrights and directors on earlier iterations of their work using his theatremaking skills to inform the structure and development of new work. He works with multi-sensory company Frozen Light who create shows for adults with profound and multiple learning disabilities (who he frequently collaborates with). He also runs workshops on accessibility through play, and treats access like a muscle, that needs to be trained more and more in order for its implementation to be at its peak.

Recent credits include: *Who Plays Who?* (Barbican and Albany); *Frankenstein* (The Hawth) and an upcoming *Marvel* voice over project.

AARIAN MEHRABANI | AARIAN / ROSS

Aarian is one of the co-founders of FlawBored and co-writer of *It's A Motherf**king Pleasure.*

Aarian trained on the BA Acting (Collaborative and devised theatre) course at the Royal Central School of Speech and Drama, graduating in 2020. Before moving to London in 2017 he worked closely with The Royal Exchange Theatre in Manchester, appearing in shows such as *Nothing* (2016/2017), directed by Bryony Shanahan and BRINK, directed by Matthew Xia.

He also works in musical theatre. Playing Aziz in Leo&Hyde's UK tour of *GUY: A New Musical* and 2021 R&D, and continues to collaborate with Leo&Hyde on their new musical *Galileo*, and working on other new musical theatre projects such as Amir Shoenfeld and Caitlyn Burt's new musical based on the life of Otto Weidt.

Most recently as an actor, he played Bun in Michael Morpurgo's *The Sleeping Sword* adapted by Tatty Hennessy, at the Watermill Theatre. He also writes and performs music under the name Aarian and his debut single *Five Yard Line* was released on all streaming services in May 2022.

In addition to his work as one of the co-founders of FlawBored he engages in a range of other freelance work including designing and delivering workshops in a range of educational and corporate settings, sitting on the steering committee for ASYLUM Arts and the audition panel for the BA Acting Program at The Royal Central School of Speech and Drama.

CHLOE PALMER | CHLOE / HELEN RICHARDSON

Chloe is one of the co-founders of FlawBored and co-writer of *It's A Motherf**king Pleasure.*

She is an actor and writer who graduated from the BA Acting Collaborative and Devised Course at Royal Central School of Speech and Drama in 2020.

As an actor: *We Need to Talk About Grief* by Sonia Jalaly, dir. Seán Linnen (Donmar Warehouse); *White Girls Gang* by Rianna Simons, dir. Babirye Bukilwa (New Diorama Theatre) and *CONTAINS ADULT THEMES AND VIOLENCE* by Martha Watson-Allpress, dir. Nat Rite (Upstairs at the Gatehouse).

As a writer Chloe has worked with Theatre Royal Stratford East and the Royal Court Theatre.

CREATIVE TEAM

JOSH ROCHE | DIRECTOR

Josh is the winner of the JMK Award 2017, the UK's most prestigious award for directors under 30, directing *My Name is Rachel Corrie* at the Young Vic, edited by Alan Rickman & Katherine Viner, starring Erin Doherty. He has directed over twenty productions, including *Pressure* by David Haig (The Royal Alexandra, Toronto); *Home* by David Storey (Chichester Festival Theatre); *Orlando* by Lucy Roslyn (59E59, New York); *Winky* by George Saunders (UK Premiere, Soho Theatre); *Radio* by Al Smith (Audible UK); *Plastic* by Kenny Emson (Poleroid Theatre) and *No Particular Order* by Joel Tan (Theatre503). In 2016 he directed the opening of the World Shakespeare Congress at the Royal Shakespeare Congress, and directed Judi Dench, Sir Ian Mckellen, Rory Kinnear, Tim Minchin, Paapa Essiedu, Benedict Cumberbatch, David Tennant, Harriet Walter and Prince Charles in the televised event *Shakespeare Live!* He was assistant director for the RSC, Shakespeare's Globe and on the West End. Josh was formerly literary associate at Soho Theatre. He is the co-founder of the national OpenHire campaign, which advocates for transparent hiring processes in UK theatre. www.joshrochedirector.com

ASYLUM ARTS | PRODUCER FOR VAULTS AND SOHO

ASYLUM Arts is a company focused on curating and promoting exceptional disabled and neurodivergent work. ASYLUM was founded in 2021 by Stephen Bailey (Royal Theatrical Support Trust Sir Peter Hall Directing Award Winner 2022). ASYLUM produces work, delivers training on neurodiverse inclusion and reinvests its profits in training for early career disabled and neurodivergent practitioners.

ASYLUM are members of Barbican Open Lab and have worked with organisations including the National Theatre, Royal Court Theatre, The Yard, Hijinx, Theatre Deli, Pentabus, and Graeae. Shows developed include *Who Plays Who* about disabled casting in Hollywood; digital production *Yoga for the Feet* by Tilly Lunken with Ellandar; *Surfacing* by Papatango Winner Tom Powell; and *That's Not My Name* by Sammy Trotman and *Covered in Jam*.

The first edition of ASYLUM Gym offered a course of learning, advocacy and practical career advancement for twenty two neurodivergent and disabled artists. It was funded by Arts Council England. ASYLUM have been supported by Unlimited, The Barbican, British Telecom, Arts Council England, Lewisham Borough of Culture and London Liberty Festival.

You can find ASYLUM @TheatreASYLUM and contasylumcic@gmail.com

HANNAH SMITH | PRODUCER

Hannah is an independent producer, currently working with The Wardrobe Ensemble, Brook Tate & FlawBored. Shows produced include: *Mog the Forgetful Cat* (The Old Vic & Royal & Derngate, Northampton); *Birthmarked* (Bristol Old Vic); *Education, Education, Education* (UK tour & West End); *1972: The Future of Sex* (UK tour).

CARA EVANS | DESIGNER

Cara (She/They) is a performance designer, an associate director at OPIA Collective and a reader at the Royal Court Theatre.

Theatre includes: as Designer or Co-Designer, *The Living Newspaper* (Royal Court Theatre); *Sleepova* (Bush Theatre); *Sirens* (Mercury Colchester Studio); *Get Dressed!* (Unicorn Theatre); *Queer Upstairs* (Royal Court Theatre); *SK Shlomo: Breathe* (Royal Albert Hall); *The Misandrist* (Arcola); *Bright Half Life* (King's Head Theatre); *It's A Motherf**king Pleasure* (Soho & Tour); *Body Show* (Soho & Pleasance); *F**king Men* (Waterloo East); *The Beach House* (Park 90); *Blanket Ban* (New Diorama/Underbelly); *Ordinary Miracle and Love Bomb* (NYT); *Instructions for a Teenage Armageddon* (Southwark Playhouse); *The Woman Who Turned Into A Tree/Refuge* (New Nordics Festival/Jackson's Lane); as Associate Designer for Chloe Lamford, *Teenage Dick* (Donmar School's Tour).

ALEX MUSGRAVE | LIGHTING DESIGNER

Alex has been nominated for an Off West End Award for Best Lighting Design for *You are Here* at the Southwark Playhouse. Alex was the recipient of the Association of Lighting Designers Lumiere Scheme. Most recent design work includes: *Home* (Chichester Festival Theatre); *Private Lives* (The Barn Theatre, Cirencester); *The Cunning Little Vixen* (Royal Birmingham Conservatoire); *Rapunzel* (Watermill Theatre); *Anyone Can Whistle* and *You Are Here* (Southwark Playhouse); *Oppenheimer* (Mountview); *King Charles III* and *Let The Right One In* (ArtsEd); *Widows* and *Sweet Smell of Success* (GSA); *Company* (Mountview).

ABI TURNER | LIGHTING DESIGNER

Abi (They/Them) is a lighting designer and access consultant. Lighting credits include: *I F**ked You In My Spaceship* (Soho Theatre); *Operation Hummingbird* (York Theatre Royal); *Pressure Drop* (Yard Theatre); *Savage Heart* (regional tour); *It's A Motherf**king Pleasure* (VAULT Festival); *Surfacing* (VAULT Festival); *A Monster Calls* (Watermill Theatre); *All the Happy Things* (Theatre503); *How Disabled Are You?* (Omnibus and Park Theatre); *A Partnership* (regional tour); *Henry V* (Donmar Warehouse and NT Live) (ALD); *Essentially Black* (Soho Theatre and Camden Peoples' Theatre) and *Milk and Gall* (Theatre 503) (ALD). Abi's access work specialises in relaxed performances, and includes consultation for companies including ASYLUM Arts, Theatre503, and in association with the National Theatre and TourettesHero.

CALUM PERRIN | SOUND DESIGNER

Calum Perrin is a composer and artist who works across theatre, performance and radio. Their recent work for theatre includes: *Ten Days in a Madhouse* (Jack Studio Theatre); *The Boys Are Kissing* (Theatre 503); *Constellations* (Vaudeville Theatre); *Risklab* (Deutsches Theater). Their recent work for radio includes: *Bells That Still Can Ring* and *Radio Waves* (BBC Radio 4); *Unread, Northumberland's Electric Coast* and *Chromophonia* (BBC Radio 3); and *The Electricity of Every Living Thing* (Audible).

DAN LIGHT | VIDEO DESIGNER

Dan Light is a video designer; based in London, working across theatre, music, and live events. Dan is the recipient of The Lord Mayors Prize (GSMD), The Paul McCartney Human Spirit Award (LIPA SFC), and was an Offies 2023 finalist.

Dan's video design credits include: *Snowflakes* (Park Theatre); *How to Break Out of A Detention Centre* (Riverside Studios); *The UK Drill Project* (Barbican Centre); *Move Fast and Break Things* (Freight Theatre); *SAD* (Omnibus Theatre); *Instructions For A Teenage Armageddon* (Southwark Playhouse); *What Do You See* (The Pappy Show).

JOSIE IRELAND | ASSOCIATE VIDEO DESIGNER

Josie Ireland is a lighting designer and theatre technician based in London, currently studying Theatre Technology at Guildhall School of Music & Drama. They work primarily with new writing and queer theatre, and particularly enjoy working in immersive and interactive experiences. Josie has a broad range of experience in a number of roles, such as Sound No.4 on *Secret Cinema: Guardians of the Galaxy* (Wembley Park). Her recent credits as lighting designer include *Autumn Opera Scenes* (GSMD); *Salt* (Theatre503) and *Impurity!* (Bishopsgate Institute), as well as assistant lighting designer on *La descente d'Orphée aux enfers* (Vache Baroque Fetival) and lighting programmer for Everyman (GSMD). Josie received the Francis Reid Award for Best Emerging Lighting Designer in 2020.

Josie's studies are made possible with the support of the Guildhall Scholarship Fund.

BEATRICE GALLOWAY | PRODUCTION STAGE MANAGER

Beatrice Galloway is a freelance Belgo-British production stage manager who trained at the Edinburgh School of Lighting, Sound and Stage Management.

Recent theatre include: *Public* (Ockham's Razor); *Famous Puppet Death Scenes* (The Old Trout Workshop); *On The Beach* (Spare Tyre); *The Cart (Oily Cart)*; *In the Weeds* (Mull Theatre); *Tank & Me* (Collectif and Then...); *Space to Be* (Oily Cart); *Unreal City* (Dream Think Speak & Access All Areas); *All Wrapped Up* (Oily Cart); *Belly of the Whale* (Ockham's Razor); *Flight Paths* (Extant).

She has also worked on exhibitions *Beasts of London* (Museum of London), events such as Glasgow Commonwealth Games 2014 and film *The Lady in the Van.*

LAUREN HASTINGS | STAGE MANAGER FOR VAULTS

Lauren Hastings is a stage manager, and recent graduate of The Royal Central School of Speech and Drama, who is currently based in London. Her recent stage work includes: *It's A Motherf**king Pleasure* by FlawBored (VAULTS), and Russell Bolam's *The Woods* (The Southwark Playhouse).

CARRIE CROFT | STAGE MANAGER FOR R&D

Carrie is a producer and production manager, based in London. Alongside freelance work, she is the resident production manager for Rose Bruford Southwest (ALRA). She completed the MA Collaborative Theatre Production and Design course at Guildhall School of Music and Drama with Distinction in 2022. Carrie is particularly interested in theatre with a socio-political message; particularly shows with historical, feminist or LGBTQ+ themes, as well as performances with accessibility and education at its core.

Recent theatre credits include: *Apocalypse Bear Trilogy* (Brockley Jack Theatre); *Disruption, Shape Of Things* (Park 200, Park Theatre); *Love and Information* (Omnibus Theatre); *Fucking Men* (Waterloo East); *Breeding* (Kings Head Theatre); *Earthquakes in London* and *Ring Ring* (Omnibus Theatre); *Under the Black Rock* (Arcola Theatre); *Sus* (Park 90, Park Theatre); *Nora: A Doll's House* and *The Ballad of Maria Martin* (Pleasance Theatre); *Three Winters* (Battersea Arts Centre); *Three Sisters* (Brixton House Theatre).

VICTORIA HOYLE | ACCESS SUPPORT FOR VAULTS, SOHO AND EDINBURGH

Victoria is an actor and freelance access worker based in London. She has enjoyed working with the actors of FlawBored since their run at VAULT Festival.

TIKA MU'TAMIR | ACCESS SUPPORT FOR R&D

Tika Mu'tamir is a dual heritage Malaysian/Northern Irish performer and community driven, devising collaborator.

They enjoy being in creative rooms that work towards inclusion, education and outreach. Tika's work takes her between Malaysia and the UK, working with and for various caring, bold and authentic theatre companies and projects.

Theatre credits: *Squirrel* (Unicorn theatre); *After the Act* (New Diorama); *The Sleeping Sword* (The Watermill); *Me & My Bee* (National Theatre River Stage Festival); *The Handlebards* (UK/International tour).

**New
Diorama
Theatre**

New Diorama Theatre is a pioneering studio venue in the heart of London.

Based on the corner of Regent's Park, over the last ten years New Diorama has been at the heart of a new movement in British theatre. New Diorama is the only venue in the UK entirely dedicated to providing a home for the country's best independent theatre companies and ensembles, and has established a national record as a trailblazer for early-career artist support.

"A genuine theatrical phenomenon – a miniature powerhouse." – *The Stage*

In 2022, New Diorama was named The Stage's Fringe Theatre Of The Year, for the second time in its short history; and in 2023 was awarded the inaugural Critics Circle Empty Space Venue Award. Since opening in 2010, New Diorama's work has also won four prestigious Peter Brook Awards; eleven Off West End Awards including Off West End Artistic Director of the Year; and The Stage's Innovation Prize.

"A must-visit destination for London theatregoers." – *Time Out*

Work commissioned and produced at New Diorama frequently tours nationally and internationally, including regular transfers Off-Broadway and co-curating New York's celebrated Brits Off Broadway Festival with 59E59 Theaters. The Stage 100, which charts power and influence across British Theatre, currently list New Diorama as the most influential independent studio theatre in the UK.

"A crucial part of the wider UK theatre ecology and an undersung hero." – *The Guardian*

In 2023, New Diorama achieved a further milestone with two original commissions transferring into London's West End. *For Black Boys Who Have Considered Suicide When The Hue Gets Too Heavy*, originally co-produced with Nouveau Riche and earning their artistic director Ryan Calais-Cameron an Olivier

Award nomination for Best New Play, transferred first to the Royal Court Theatre before a limited, sell-out West End run at the Apollo Theatre. Alongside, *Operation Mincemeat*, an original New Diorama commission from musical theatre company Spitlip, transferred to the Fortune Theatre, where it has already extended its run several times.

"New Diorama has only been around for a decade but has already left a huge mark on the global theatre scene." – *WhatsOnStage*

www.newdiorama.com | @NewDiorama | New Diorama Theatre, 15-16 Triton Street, Regent's Place, London NW1 3BF.

UNTAPPED

UNDERBELLY | NEW DIORAMA THEATRE
CONCORD THEATRICALS | NOUVEAU RICHE

Originally developed in 2018 by New Diorama and Underbelly to discover and support emerging theatre makers at the Edinburgh Festival Fringe, the Untapped Award has established a remarkable record as a platform for bold new theatre by outstanding companies.

Over its 2018, 2019 and 2022 editions, the first three years of the Untapped Award have already provided a springboard for major Edinburgh Fringe premieres. Previous recipients have gone on to win three Fringe First Awards *This is Not a Show About Hong Kong* (Max Percy & Friends); *It's True, It's True, It's True* (Breach); *Dressed* (ThisEgg) and a Stage Edinburgh Award *Queens of Sheba* (Nouveau Riche). Winners have also gone on to secure major national and international tours following the festival (including Burnt Lemon's *Tokyo Rose*, Ugly Bucket's *Good Grief* and *Queens of Sheba*, which most recently played at New York's Public Theater for the prestigious Under the Radar Festival, and adaptations for screen, with *It's True, It's True, It's True* broadcast on BBC television.

"The Untapped trio ranked among the best of the entire festival, proof that support from organisations like Underbelly and New Diorama can pay off in spades." – *WhatsOnStage*

For 2023, the award was relaunched and super-charged with support from new partners Concord Theatricals and previous winners Nouveau Riche, with the cash investment in each company doubled to £10,000 alongside an extensive paid-for support package and publication by Concord Theatricals under their UK imprint Samuel French Ltd.

Drawn from a nationwide talent search receiving a record one hundred and eighty submissions, the three 2023 winners are *Dugsi Dayz* by Side eYe, a Somali remix of *The Breakfast Club*; *One Way Out* by No Table Productions, a dynamic drama about young British Caribbeans' experiences of the Windrush crisis; and *It's A Motherf**king Pleasure* by FlawBored, a scathing satire on identity politics which asks "What if disabled people were out to make as much money as possible from the guilt of non-disabled, anxious people (like you)?"

CHARACTERS

SAM / TIM – Blind or visually impaired performer
CHLOE / HELEN RICHARDSON – female identifying performer
AARIAN / ROSS – Blind or visually impaired, performer of colour, who is preferably queer

AUTHOR'S NOTES

This play was written to be a fun, contemporaneous satire that pokes fun at the monetisation of identity politics. The play is written to highlight the idea of able anxiety, and to portray disabled characters as being capable of cruelty, manipulation and greed. So any production of this play should have the same ideas at it's heart. Use them as your north star for your production.

This script is intended as a play for three people.

Performer 1 – **SAM** and **TIM**
Performer 2 – **CHLOE** and **HELEN RICHARDSON**
Performer 3 – **AARIAN** and **ROSS**

All other parts may be allocated as you see fit. We would suggest, but not insist, that you change the character names of Beatrice, **AARIAN**, **CHLOE** and **SAM** to the names of your company.

Though the names may change, the parts of **AARIAN** and **SAM** must be performed by blind or visually impaired performers, and the part of **CHLOE** must be played by a female identifying performer.

The part of **AARIAN** should be played by a performer of colour, who is preferably queer...but obviously don't ask people who they're sleeping with in an audition.

All performances of this play must be captioned throughout.

No visual jokes should be added to the production, as they will not be audio described.

Certain aspects of the text should be changed according to the context of your production.

Any text that is in **bold**, and occurs between the word (**a**) – **for adaptable** and (**f**) – **for fixed** indicates text that can be changed. (The letters are included in brackets so that anyone using a screen reader can access the script). This is usually audio description, or details that were contemporaneous to the writing of the play. These should be replaced with details that are relevant to your company's experience of ableism, or relevant to your production and your company. If you can't find any examples of ableism, congratulations, the world is fixed.

All lines ascribed to **JOHN** are unspoken captioned text.

SD denotes a stage direction.

(i) indicates an interruption and the point at which the next line begins.

... indicates that the thought trails off.

Enjoy!

With thanks to:

Arts Council England
David Ralf and all of the team at Theatre Deli
Soho Theatre
Vault Festival
David Byrne and the team at New Diorama
Underbelly
Camden People's Theatre
Greenwich Theatre
Wildcard
Watermill Theatre
Pleasance
Jamie Hale and the team at CRIPtic Arts
Maria Oshodi and the team at Extant
Something for the Weekend
Kate Wyver

Dedicated to Eddie Redmayne

Scene One

(**SAM**, **AARIAN**, *and* **CHLOE** *enter, led by* **SAM**.)

SAM. Hi everyone, we're (**a**) **FlawBored** (**f**). Thank you for coming to our performance of *It's A Motherf**king Pleasure*. I'm Sam.

CHLOE. Hi I'm Chloe.

AARIAN. Hi I'm Aarian. Before we begin, we wanted to mention that Sam and I are legally blind and as we're a disability-led theatre company, one of the big things for us is making sure that audiences are able to access our work. An example of this is self-description so vision-impaired audience members are aware of what we look like.

So, I'm a (**a**) **six-foot middle-eastern man with thick black hair and a shaved face. I'm wearing a pink jacket, blue jeans, and white shoes** (**f**).

SAM. (**a**) **I'm a six-foot-one white man with a shaved head and a short ginger beard. I'm wearing a dark navy suit and a light-green shirt** (**f**).

CHLOE. (**a**) **I'm a five-foot-eight white woman with blonde hair, blue eyes, and freckles. I'm wearing a blue shirt, grey trousers, and trainers** (**f**).

SAM. Before we start the show, we want this space to be as accessible and inclusive as possible. We base the way that we work on the social model of disability. Hands up if you've heard of the social model of disability.

(Beat.)

I can't see any hands.

Haha. Sorry, just a little blind joke. So, uh social model, which basically means: I, as Sam, am not disabled, society disables me. I have an impairment and the world around me is disabling me. An example of this practically is, well, I know because of my vision impairment my retinas react poorly to bright light so I need the lights lowered a bit so I can distinguish who the people are in the playing area of the stage. This makes it safer for me.

(*SD – Directed to the tech box:*)

So, Beatrice? Can I have the lights just dimmed a little bit?

(*SD – The lights dim.*)

Thanks.

AARIAN. You might also notice the black and yellow tape along the edges of the carpet, this is so I can see the edge of the stage and don't bump into you.

(*SD –* **SAM** *and* **AARIAN** *assemble the set as* **CHLOE** *speaks.*)

CHLOE. As the sighted member of the company, I'm going to audio describe the set to you. **(a) So, Sam and Aarian are moving two microphone stands into position stage right. They are also moving two comfy white chairs and a small side table into position stage left. On the floor we have a yellow carpet which is secured with black and yellow tape**.

At the back there is a screen for projected video and there are captions (f).

So those are all just examples of our way of working because we thought it'd be good to share the way we work. Now obviously Sam and Aarian have shared their access needs, and you all should have been asked by the venue *(SD – She begins to take out a piece of paper from her pocket)* if you have any access needs for this show. Now obviously we don't want to out anyone, this is about creating a safe space for you.

AARIAN & SAM. *(SD – Mumbled.)* Absolutely not.

CHLOE. So don't worry, we won't use names. But we do know that the person in D5 needs a bit more light to engage with the show. So Beatrice, can we get a spotlight on D5 please?

(SD – Spotlight on D5.)

Is that better D5? Great. As I said, we don't want to out anyone. The reason we have put more light there is so that the person in D5 can have equitable access to the show.

AARIAN. Now we also know that the person sitting in B8 lipreads so we've arranged for Sam to face them for the rest of the performance.

(SD – **SAM** *takes one of the chairs and positions himself directly in front of B8. He is uncomfortably close and all of his lines are now over articulated to the person in B8.)*

CHLOE. And the person in E2 is hard of hearing so needs us to speak a little louder for clarity during this show, so we will be projecting a bit more in a smaller space.

(SD – From now on the lines are half-shouted.)

SAM. There are captions that will be saying what we say as we go along. This is for audience members who might need some clarity in the speech and for our D/deaf audience members.

CHLOE. We also know that some people in row C might have a negative reaction to loud noises, so we are providing some earplugs. Sam, give them the earplugs.

(SD – **SAM** *pulls the earplugs out of his pocket and passes them out to the audience while* **AARIAN** *and* **CHLOE** *consult the list 'what's next?')*

SAM. Yeah, so we tend to adapt these shows depending on the audience we have so it's not an 'equal sharing' it's an equitable sharing. So, the difference between equal and equitable is if... well let's take a race, equal means that everyone starts from the same place whereas equitable means everyone starts from the place they need to be (i).

AARIAN. Sam?

SAM. Yeah?

CHLOE. We just realised that because you weren't facing B8 from the beginning, they won't have got the social model of disability bit, so we think you should start again.

(Beat.)

SAM. Hi everyone, I'm a (**a**) **six-foot-one white man with a shaved head and a short ginger beard, we're FlawBored** (**f**). Thank you for coming to our performance of *It's a Motherf**king Pleasure.*

AARIAN. So, for those who consider themselves non-disabled.

(SD – **CHLOE** *finds someone in the audience.)*

CHLOE. Non-disabled? Non-disabled? OK, great!

(SD – **CHLOE** *directs* **AARIAN** *to the person she has found and they both stand directly in front of them. Throughout this* **SAM** *keeps losing his place and repeatedly checks the captions to work out what's next.)*

AARIAN. You are in a position of privilege and you need to check that privilege because you have more access to the show than others (i) so what we're gonna do.

    (SD – To B8:)

SAM. So how many people have heard of the social model of disability? Could you raise your hands? I can't see any hands…Haha. Sorry, just a little blind joke.

CHLOE. So, if you don't mind, please stand up and face the back for the first half of the show, we will let you know when to turn around again.

    (SD – To B8:)

SAM. So, uh social model which basically means: I, as Sam am not disabled, society disables me. So, Beatrice? Can I have the lights just dimmed a little bit?

    (SD – The lights dim again.)

CHLOE. We understand the importance of touch tours for some audience members. So, I am going to pass Aarian around the front row.

    *(SD – **CHLOE** directs **AARIAN** to the front row. **AARIAN** is placed in front of an audience member with his arms outstretched to the side, encouraging them to touch him.)*

AARIAN. If somebody can audio describe what they are feeling for those not in the front row.

CHLOE. If you don't want to touch him just don't, we just want to make sure that the option is there. So, it's more 'equitable not equal'.

    *(SD – Throughout this **AARIAN** has been asking people what they feel.)*

AARIAN. Uncomfortable? This person says they're feeling uncomfortable.

*(SD – **CHLOE** runs up to **AARIAN** and moves him along one audience member.)*

CHLOE. So as Sam said earlier there are captions at the back of the stage, and they'll be repeating what we say.

(SD – She looks at the captions and notices that they are a bit behind:)

Hold up they're a bit behind.

*(SD – Meanwhile **AARIAN** is sidestepping along the front row, encouraging each audience member to touch him. Occasionally, **AARIAN** turns so that his back is to the audience allowing them to touch both sides of him.)*

JOHN. Hold up they're a bit behi... *(SD – All captions clear off the screen.)* What the fuck is going on?

CHLOE. I'll just read this out for any visually-impaired audience members. The captions just said, "what the fuck is going on?" Can we go back to the script please, John? *(SD – To the audience.)* John is the captioner.

JOHN. Can we go back to the script please, John? John is the captioner.

CHLOE. The captions are currently saying "John is the captioner". Can we get back to the script please, John?

JOHN. The captions are currently saying "John is the captioner". Can we get back to the script please, John?

No.

CHLOE. John says "No".

SAM. What the fuck John.

JOHN. What the fuck John.

CHLOE. The captions are saying "What the fuck John".

JOHN. It usually doesn't go as bad as this.

(*SD –* **SAM** *comes up close to read them.*)

SAM. John is saying "it usually doesn't go as bad as this" (i).

CHLOE. (i) Shut up Sam.

JOHN. Shut up Sam.

SAM. The captions now say "Shut up Sam".

AARIAN. (*SD – from the front row.*) Sam! You need to face B8!

JOHN. This is what happens when you're given five days to caption a whole show.

SAM. (*SD – Reading captions.*) This is what happens when you're given five days to caption a whole show.

(*SD –* **AARIAN** *abandons the touch tour.*)

AARIAN. So, trigger warnings. We don't want to give anything away but there are some gay jokes. If you are sensitive to that, the earplugs are in Row C. So, whoever ended up with the earplugs please watch out for gay people around you.

JOHN. I'll start again.

SAM. (*SD – Reading captions.*) I'll start again.

CHLOE. Women! We are underrepresented on stage, there are two men and one of me. But don't worry, we all agreed that Beatrice and I would get paid (**a**) **thirty seven percent** (**f**) more to address the gender (i) pay gap.

JOHN. Hi everyone we're (**a**) **FlawBored** (**f**). The social model of disability is where I'm disabled and for me, I need that light (i) a little lower –

SAM. (*SD – Reading captions.*) Hi everyone we're (**a**) **FlawBored** (**f**). The social model of disability is where

I'm disabled and for me, I need that light (i) a little lower –

(SD – The lights dim again.)

CHLOE. Obviously we want this show to be carbon neutral, so you can join us later for a little shrub planting ceremony. We will be planting two shrubs for (**a**) **Sam because, as an Australian (f)**, his carbon footprint is (i) fucking massive.

AARIAN. We do need the earplugs back at the end of the show. So whichever gay ends up with them, please leave the earplugs, along with your number, with the usher on (i) your way out.

JOHN. Hi everyone we're (**a**) **FlawBored (f)**. The social model of disability is where I'm disabled and for me, I need that light a (i) little lower –

SAM. *(Reading captions.)* Hi everyone we're (**a**) **FlawBored (f)**. The social model of disability is where I'm disabled and for me, I need that light a (i) little lower –

(SD – The lights dim again.)

CHLOE. As one of the two white members of the company, we also wanted to acknowledge Aarian's (**a**) **Iranian (f)** heritage, so I'd like to take a moment to say to Aarian and the group (**a**) **"Salaam, Haal e toon. Chetoreh" (f)**.

(**a**) **Salaam, Haal e toon. Chetoreh is captioned in Farsi (f)**.

JOHN. Hi everyone we're (**a**) **FlawBored (f)**.

SAM. *(SD – Reading captions.)* Hi everyone we're (**a**) **FlawBored (f)**.

AARIAN. (**a**) **Salaam. Man khoobam, merci**.

Salaam. Man khoobam, merci is also captioned in Farsi (f).

JOHN. The social model of disability is where I'm disabled and for me, I need that light a little lower –

SAM. *(SD – Reading captions.)* The social model of disability is where I'm disabled and for me, I need that light a little lower –

> *(SD – The lights have now dimmed so much that we end up in a blackout.)*

Scene Two

(Lights up.)

SAM. We're starting in a boardroom. Cue a hybrid soundscape of office sounds.

(SD – The sounds begin.)

We're in a boardroom inside a fictional PR talent management agency called RIZE with a Z. Their goal, to turn people into influential brands...putting the **(a) Disney into Walt, the Kardashian into Kim, the Ye into Kanye (f)** ...you know scum. There's been an 'incident.' One of their top grossing influencers has 'done an ableism'. Very publicly. RIZE with a Z is in crisis mode, or back-pedalling if you will. On stage right is Aarian at a microphone, to his left is Chloe also at a microphone. What the sighted audience can't see is that I'm going to be standing offstage eating a banana.

> *(SD – **SAM** leaves and eats a banana offstage.*
> ***CHLOE** and **AARIAN** are on microphones. In our version: **CHLOE** played **LISA**, **GEORGIA** and **HELEN**. **AARIAN** played **PAUL** and **CINDY**. It's not important who plays what voices but whoever plays **HELEN** in the show must play **HELEN** in this scene. The characters are all caricatures. This should be short, snappy and fast.)*

LISA. Paul good to see you. Apologies everyone for the short notice. I got here as soon as I could. Could someone (i) please.

PAUL. I'm Paul!

LISA. Not Paul. Can someone explain this to me? Ms Richardson please.

HELEN. Hi, Helen Richardson, HR. Well, we've come across a challenge, the firm as you know is doing a considerable amount of business every day...and as you know our clients are our clients because of their own unique voice who will often (i).

LISA. Somebody please explain this to me succinctly.

CINDY. Well...I...work for risk management under Ms Richardson. And as I'm sure you know; over the last few years we have seen an uptick in desire to hear from more diverse clients (i).

LISA. Will someone please just say what has happened.

GEORGIA. We are, at present, being called discriminatory.

LISA. Thank you! To whom am I speaking?

> *(SD – **SAM** re-enters with a half-eaten banana.)*

SAM. Sorry, Sam here just with a bit of audio description info. I just want to point out that Chloe and Aarian are attempting to play multiple characters through the microphones...we've tried to distinguish this through simple stuff like maybe a slight shift in the way a character might speak in terms of rhythm or pitch... but we're also aware that Chloe and Aarian don't have particularly good range as actors. So if that's making the scene inaccessible for you, we're sorry...John was very clear that we had to explain and apologise for this to our D/deaf audience members. Great.

GEORGIA. I'm Georgia. I'm your crisis management consultant.

LISA. Georgia. Speak to me. Who are we 'perceived' as being discriminatory to?

GEORGIA. We're being accused of 'ableism'.

LISA. And that is?

GEORGIA. It's a form of discrimination against people with disabilities or who are perceived to be disabled (i). Ableism characterises people –

LISA. I understand.

HELEN. Hi, sorry, Helen Richardson, HR. We already have several responses ready to go. I have already drafted an apology that we can release.

PAUL. Now Helen, that'd be a great idea. Except for the fact that these people can't read. Let's not rub salt into the wound.

LISA. Helen, though Paul's sarcasm isn't the most professional, I am beginning to understand his frustration with you. Who are you?

TIM. Uhh, Tim.

> *(SD –* **AARIAN** *and* **CHLOE** *move away from the microphones.)*

AARIAN. Meet Tim.

CHLOE. Played by Sam.

AARIAN. So, because Tim is a recurring character in the story, we're going to do something new, which we're quite excited about called 'Integrated, Creative Audio Description'...or ICAD.

CHLOE. Don't need the (i) acronym.

AARIAN. To give visually-impaired audiences a truly accurate picture of the character, we're going to describe not just the physical appearance, but the *vibe* his physical appearance is giving off. So, for example, the vibe I'm getting is kind of...white supremacist.

CHLOE. Yeah, great, but I think because he's in a suit he's like on his way back from court.

AARIAN. Yeah, yeah yeah, like he's just been tried for GBH, but he got released cos there was insufficient evidence.

CHLOE. And he's got this semi gormless look on his face like, like...he's just taken an edible.

AARIAN. OK amazing so we've got a skinhead white supremacist on his way out of court for GBH who's just taken an edible...that's his Integrated Creative Audio Description.

CHLOE. He's also a junior agent at RIZE.

AARIAN. And he's blind.

CHLOE. Yeah, he was a diversity hire and no one really takes him seriously but now, he's seen his opportunity.

> (*SD –* **AARIAN** *and* **CHLOE** *move back to the microphones.*)

LISA. Who are you?

TIM. ummmm Tim and...ummm... Well...uh... I'm... actually (i) disabled myself...and uh.

LISA. Speak up.

TIM. I'm blind.

> (*Beat.*)

LISA & PAUL. (*SD – Mutterings.*) Oh fuck (i) Oh Jesus Christ.

> (*Beat.*)

LISA. Tell us your thoughts.

TIM. We need to stop predicting cultural trends and create them instead.

> (*Beat.*)

LISA. Go on.

TIM. What if we make this the next moral purity test.

HELEN. Hi Tim, I – oh, sorry, Helen Richardson here, HR. Whilst I totally understand and hear your lived experience... I...um... I wonder if maybe this type of action might come across as (i) disingenuous...

TIM. What I'm trying to say is that we can make disability the next cultural cachet people scramble for. Imagine where RIZE would be if we had been the company that ignited the #MeToo movement.

    (Beat.)

I've got someone in mind. He's blind, he's gay, he's brown...he's perfect.

PAUL. Lisa, that's called intersectionality.

LISA. I'm aware.

Okay Tim, I'm willing to roll the dice. Georgia, I'd like you to create a pitch (i).

TIM. Sorry...I think I should be leading this one.

LISA. Why?

TIM. Well, disabled voices should represent disabled voices.

LISA & PAUL. *(SD – ashamedly.)* Oh yes of course, I'm sorry (i). Oh yes of course, exactly, I never said that that wasn't even me.

TIM. And anyway, you've already got me. Make the most of it.

    (SD – Silence.)

LISA. Georgia?

GEORGIA. Sounds like a good idea.

LISA. Helen?

HELEN. Um...

LISA. Paul?

PAUL. Well my nephew is gay (i).

LISA. Very well Tim, you've got 'til the end of the week.

Scene Three

JOHN. Scene three. Tim's office.

SAM. The captions say Scene three, Tim's office. Soooo… here's a bit of audio description, so you know where we are…we're in a different place…but it's still the same set. We're in an office and it's like…it's grey. There's ummmm heating, but that's also grey – the radiators are – well they're more of an off-white – a beige, an off-beige…but the grey, ummm the grey is like a…umm…a grey…grey…sky, there's pipes which are uh…also grey like rain clouds or grey clouds when it's just cloudy…

(Beat.)

Look, I don't know man…I can't fucking see.

HELEN. Uh knock knock.

TIM. Ah Helen how may (i) I.

HELEN. Hi Tim, this is Helen Richardson HR here (i).

TIM. Yes Helen I (i) know who.

HELEN. I'm a **(a) five-foot-eight white woman with (i) short wavy blonde hair (f)**.

TIM. **(a) Short wavy blonde hair (f)**, thank you Helen… what can I help (i) you with?

HELEN. Your turn.

TIM. I'm sorry?

HELEN. Your turn Tim…your self-description.

(SD – The scene snaps into 'ICAD' mode.)

AARIAN. This is Helen Richardson.

SAM. Played by Chloe.

AARIAN. Her Integrated Creative Audio Description is... well she's (**a**) **white woman** (**f**). Is that clear enough?

SAM. Yeah, she's so concerned about not offending anyone that she's not been able to pass a stool in three weeks.

AARIAN. She's like a six-month-old poodle who's just been washed with human shampoo and even though her skin feels like it's burning from the inside out, she still wants to show her owner that she's appreciative.

> *(SD – Back to office.)*

HELEN. Self-description Timothy...we learnt about it during the workshop.

TIM. There was a workshop?

HELEN. Yes.

TIM. Right.

HELEN. Well...

> *(Beat.)*

TIM. I'm a (**a**) **six-foot-one white man with a shaved head and a short ginger beard** (**f**).

HELEN. Thank you. Now Tim, I thought I'd catch you before you meet this new wonderboy (i).

TIM. Ross (i).

HELEN. Yes. I wanted you to know that I've told everyone in the office that when meeting Ross it is important for them to see the person, not the condition.

TIM. I'm not sure (i) that you need to explain.

HELEN. Ross is more than his disability. People who are blind or partially sighted, like you, still have skills to offer just like everyone else.

(SD – The line above should be typed in the captions as if it has been lifted directly from the internet...because it has.)

AARIAN. Hi Aarian here, just wanted to point out that what Helen said has been typed into the captions as if it's been lifted directly from a disability awareness site on the internet...because it has.

(SD – Back to the scene:)

HELEN. Just because they are blind does not mean they don't have value.

TIM. Mm.

HELEN. OK great. So, if you are showing him around the office, I need to show you the correct way to guide him.

TIM. Well I don't (i) think that's going to be necessary.

HELEN. OK, so for the purposes of this I will be Ross (i).

TIM. You're going to pretend to be blind?

HELEN. Tim don't be ridiculous, I'm not pretending to be blind.

(SD – Snap:)

CHLOE. OK, Chloe here, just quickly, at no point in this am I pretending to be blind. Nor am I suggesting that it's OK to play blind if you're not (i) blind.

SAM. *(SD – With haste.)* No, that would be appropriation and we wouldn't do that (i).

CHLOE. This is a miscommunication designed (i) to.

SAM. Yeah, to make (i) clear that.

CHLOE. Make clear the knots that people get into when they're (i) trying.

SAM. In good faith (i).

CHLOE. To explain themselves around these issues which *are* difficult.

(*Beat.*)

Don't tweet about me.

OK.

SAM. OK.

CHLOE. Back to the scene.

(*SD – Snap:*)

TIM. OK.

HELEN. OK so, as I'm sure you know, you must first approach and ask if it is OK to touch Ross. You must never go up to a blind person and just start touching them.

TIM. OK.

HELEN. Ask me.

(*SD – Beat. He sighs.*)

TIM. Do you want to be touched?

HELEN. Not like that!

TIM. Sorry sorry, then like how, like how Helen?

HELEN. Introduce yourself and ask, is it OK if I touch you?

TIM. Hello, I'm Tim. Is it OK if I touch you?

HELEN. Hello Tim, I'm Ross. Yes, it is OK. Touch me.

Scene Four

AARIAN. Scene four, the next day, Tim's office again.

CHLOE. Meet Ross.

SAM. Played by Aarian.

> *(Beat.)*

He's got the demeanour of a rent boy who's not managed to get a client since New Year's Eve.

CHLOE. He's built like a ruler, but not so straight.

SAM. He's like a malnourished child who somehow shops at Harrods.

CHLOE. His sense of self-confidence and self-worth are just as fragile and brittle as his scrawny little arms.

SAM. He's got the sort of face that is just crying out to be punched.

CHLOE. Oh my God you're right…it is…what's that about?

SAM. Anyway, Ross is an up-and-coming blind influencer.

CHLOE. He's been called in to meet with Tim, who he eventually finds in his very grey, office.

> *(SD – Snap:)*

TIM. I can't tell you what to do.

ROSS. No, no, I'm just sort of…wondering what sort of direction you want to push me in?

TIM. Well, that's depends on you. We like to be hands-on with the clients, but the hands are being led by the client.

ROSS. I'm not quite sure (i) I'm following.

TIM. What made you start making content in the first place?

ROSS. Well, I wanted to show people things about me. I'm bubbly, I'm fun, I'm quirky.

    (Beat.)

TIM. Is there anything else about you that's...unique?

    (Beat.)

ROSS. I drink oat milk.

    (Beat.)

TIM. Is there anything that separates you from the other people who drink oat milk?

ROSS. I guess I do it for dietary reasons rather than ethical ones.

TIM. OK, let's cut the crap.

ROSS. (a) **I've got a mole on my neck (f)**.

    (Beat.)

TIM. You can't see.

ROSS. I can't see.

TIM. Right.

ROSS. And is that why I'm here?

TIM. What? No, not just that. Although, it does provide a unique perspective, a fresh one, an interesting one.

    *(SD – **ROSS** doesn't reply.)*

And it's still you, it's just a part of you.

    *(SD – **ROSS** doesn't reply.)*

You're still the star, you're just a blind star.

ROSS. Whatever.

TIM. Come on, think of all the things we could do for good with this kind of material, maybe some nice awareness work?

ROSS. Awareness doesn't really do it for me.

TIM. Doesn't really do it (i) for you.

ROSS. I mean, I'm not like...I'm not opposed to it, but I'm not like *fuck yeah*, into it, you know?

TIM. OK.

ROSS. I don't want to be a blind influencer. I want to be an influencer who happens to be blind.

TIM. Sure.

ROSS. I do.

TIM. I know. I get it. Honestly, I do. I just want to spell out, for a couple of minutes, another track. If that's alright?

RIZE is a company with deep pockets. Our operating budget runs into the hundreds of millions, and senior management is willing to put all that cash behind you because they're feeling guilty.

They hate feeling guilty. They hate it. It pops their bubble of nobility; means they can't go conscience-free shopping or hire their nephew as their tax advisor. They are terrified of being called racist, sexist, homophobic... and now they've got a crisis manager telling them that they're ableist, and they have no fucking idea what that word means.

You've met Helen. She comes out in hives every time she says, "I'll see you later".

'Able anxiety'. We've got a lot of able anxiety out there, and we've got a lot of cash through ad deals, we just need to work out how we get from one to the other. So, what I'm asking is: What do these people want from you? What do non-disabled, guilty people like about you?

ROSS. They like boring shit, because they're boring people. They're fascinated by the mundanity of our lives because they can't wrap their heads around how we can possibly...tie our shoelaces, or cross the road without assistance.

TIM. So, we film you doing boring mundane stuff.

ROSS. I'd rather play in traffic.

TIM. I know, I know, but look, this is the version of you that makes money. You can carry on being bubbly, fun, quirky Ross and be poor, or you can be this guy, and I can pay you two thousand pounds for brushing your teeth.

(SD – Beat. ROSS still seems unconvinced.)

Hot yoga.

ROSS. Yeah (i).

TIM. That's bullshit right?

ROSS. No idea.

TIM. What about yoga in the dark?

ROSS. Tim, that's not the same as being (i) blind.

TIM. I know, I know, but we can definitely convince young millennial mothers that doing yoga in the dark is better for their pelvic floor.

(SD – ROSS smiles. TIM is spit-balling.)

Ummm...dark gyms. No more body shaming.

(SD – ROSS smiles again.)

Blind pubs and bars. Because when you can't see, you're truly listening.

(SD – ROSS laughs.)

ROSS. Nobody listens like a blind person.

TIM. Yes Ross! "Nobody listens like a blind person".

ROSS. Shopping in the dark? I dunno.

TIM. No that's great, we're releasing them from consumerism. What if we give them a breather, a day off?

ROSS. What do you (i) mean?

TIM. You're a non-disabled, straight, white, middle-class man with a steady job and...I dunno, a forty k salary.

ROSS. OK.

TIM. It's tragic.

ROSS. Why?

TIM. You've got nothing to complain about.

> *(Beat.)*

So, with us, they can...y'know.

ROSS. What?

TIM. Feel marginalised. Paddle in the shallow end of the blind swimming pool.

ROSS. They won't do that.

TIM. Yes, they will, Ross. Because you, you big blind bastard, will be telling them it's OK.

ROSS. Tim, I do not feel comfortable (i) with that.

TIM. Listen. You're thinking about this all wrong. Don't do it *for* them. Take their money because they're idiots. If the fucking lemmings want to get in line, let them. You're not providing a service. This is financial compensation for emotional labour.

> *(SD – A moment.)*

ROSS. OK, look...and I'm not saying I think we should because...well anyway, but if we did, how would we...

Scene Five

TIM. Good afternoon, everyone, thank you all for joining me.

JOHN. Scene five, the boardroom, RIZE offices.

CHLOE. *(SD – Very fast.)* The captions say Scene five: Boardroom RIZE offices. Audio description: Top of a six-floor building in north Soho just south of Oxford Street, outside the room a view onto an urban park, cirrus clouds gather overhead on a cold day, mid-March. Inside, elephant's breath carpets in a glass panelled room with Crittall doors into a communal work space, ceiling panelled grey squares, burnt copper tabletop on a large oblong table with six table legs, twelve water glasses and one speaker phone, the diffused scent (i) is mountain mist and Ohfuckhe'sstartednevermind.

TIM. My father took me on a fishing trip once in Jervis Bay. My father had a policy, it didn't matter how good your fishing rod was, it was about the quality of the bait. I remember being six, standing there, the cool breeze of the sea blowing in my face as the thirty-degree sun warmed my body, the wooden planks of the wharf underneath my feet. The sound of the current...

Other fishermen used worms, I asked my father why we weren't using worms and he told me to *look again.* Whilst the other fishermen were struggling to catch even a single fish, my father was pulling schools of them out of the water. He was always learning, always looking back at what had been done to see what *could* be done.

He used grasshoppers.

(SD – Laughs at himself.) Why am I talking about fish? Well, my father had asked me to look again, to rediscover, to relearn. Over the last few years we at *RIZE* have had to do some relearning ourselves, God knows

I have. I'm very grateful for that. These company-wide re-learnings have only been made possible because of individuals sharing their visceral lived experiences.

Visceral coming from the Latin 'visceralis'. Meaning internal.

So, I'm here with a question. What has been the main way that publicity companies like *ours* have made money in the last five years?

Trailblazers, and their lived experiences.

> *(SD – As they are mentioned they appear in a projection behind him.*)*

Colin Kaepernick.

Elliot Page.

Greta Thunberg.

But what's difficult about these people? What's turning their quest for inclusion, somehow, into exclusion?

Simple.

We can't all be black, we can't all be trans, we can't all be children.

But we can *all* be disabled.

ReVision. Because when the lights go out. We're all blind.

OK, let's get into it.

Meet Ross. He's a visually impaired, LGBTQPIAP+ person of colour.

But Ross isn't really a person. Ross is a conduit.

---

* A licence to produce IT'S A MOTHERF**KING PLEASURE does not include a performance license for any third-party or copyrighted recordings. Licensees should create their own.

Ross allows us to travel back and forth inbetween different dimensions of experience.

Imagine you're having a shower; you're thinking of everything that has happened that day. The aches and pains, the wins and the losses, you're not thinking about the here and now. Until you turn the lights out.

ReVision Cleanse.

Now you can feel the hot water hitting your skin, you can hear the sound of the dripping water touch the acrylic flooring of that shower. The water is wetter, the steam is softer, the cleanse is deeper. That becomes a memory. That becomes your Jervis Bay.

ReVision Social.

A series of in-person networking events in the dark. Meet the people behind the mask, get past the visual. Dark networking is a truly radical take on forming business and social relationships. Everyone talks more when the lights are out and remember, nobody listens like a blind person.

Dating with ReVise.

We like to pretend that looks aren't everything, but we live in a visual world where you are visually judged. ReVise is a dating app where there are no photos. Tailored matchings with people whose data matches yours, whose taste matches yours, whose experience matches yours. Wake up and smell the roses.

And last but not least, ReVision Experiences.

Blind canes offered to people as part of a week-long experience of not seeing. Feel the harsh wind of ableism. Experience a daily micro-aggression. Join the fight for your rights to access. Imagine if you too could get that seat on the tube. Aren't you tired of feeling lucky? Aren't you tired of your own privilege? With ReVision, we're taking marginalised identities mainstream, we're opening up the exclusive inclusive identities, for everyone.

Scene Six

CHLOE. OK, hi, Chloe here, so the idea for this next bit is that it all happens in the dark so that sighted members of the audience can consider their access needs when it comes to watching theatre. Aarian's got some audio description for us as well, so that you can visualise internally the space we're creating for you.

(SD – LX – Q35 – Blackout.)

AARIAN. *(SD – Starts hesitant, figuring it out and then finds a flow and gets carried away.)* OK, so... We find ourselves...in a montage... Audio Description SND - Q31: In this space, time both stands still and lives in its entirety, by which I mean that everything that is happening at this present moment in the world is contained within this one space, alongside everything that has happened and everything that is yet to happen. We are both everywhere and nowhere, together, and apart, con (i) nected and isolated. It's both as complex as a space can be and as simple as an empty room. Out of this absence...creativity, imagination. Art.

CHLOE. OK, so, hope you enjoyed that. If you're not a theatre aficionado, what happened just then was a 'meta-theatrical gesture'. That makes this show an accessible, inclusive, meta-satire, which makes us both eligible for the Total Theatre Award and gives us a much better chance of touring in Europe after the festival is over. OK great. Over to you Sam.

(SD – Montage music begins.*)

---

* A licence to produce IT'S A MOTHERF**KING PLEASURE does not include a performance license for any third-party or copyrighted music. Licensees should create an original composition or use music in the public domain. For further information, please see the Music Use Note on page iii.

SAM. So here's how ReVision became a success. First off, RIZE dealt with their Ableist oopsie in the way most places do. An organised internal review, published apologies, yada yada. It looks good and is quickly buried on the backend of their website.

CHLOE. Meanwhile, Helen now has a reading list in her email signature and everyone at RIZE is petrified of doing or saying the wrong thing.

AARIAN. Ross and Tim's first audience is mainly made up out of kids who are losing their sight and wanna watch something to make them feel less alone.

SAM. And their parents who feel lost and terrified.

AARIAN. And seriously, genuinely, this happens all the time.

SAM. All the time.

CHLOE. By proxy, they also reach the friends of these parents who are neither lost nor terrified, but who love to share pity-porn on their WhatsApp group.

> *(SD – Lights up on* **SAM**, *doing an impression of these kinds of people.)*

SAM. Oh my god, oh my God…really makes you think how privileged we are and really puts our problems into perspective… Maeve come watch this, if you don't watch this we are *not* going kite surfing.

> *(SD – Blackout.)*

AARIAN. Then Ross called out Tesco's for not allowing his guide dog into the store.

CHLOE. Even though it was just a random Labrador.

SAM. That gained some press. Article in (**a**) ***The Guardian*** (**f**), people reaching out for interviews, advice, collaborations.

AARIAN. But Ross was being careful not to become an activist.

CHLOE. Activism. Famously, not lucrative.

SAM. Now the parents are hooked, the next target is a teen audience.

CHLOE. And RIZE has a blueprint for this.

AARIAN. See they've already got a bunch of clients with young, established, impressionable audiences. So, they just stick Ross next to them and get them to act like friends. The person chosen for Ross to hang out with was Polly.

SAM. Polly is awful, she's ableist and just really really...

AARIAN. White and basic.

*(SD – Lights up on **POLLY**.)*

POLLY. Do you wanna like feel my face?

(SD – Blackout.)

SAM. With that out of the way they moved onto phase two, brand deals.

AARIAN. Brand deals give credibility.

SAM. The illusion of success.

CHLOE. And they bring in money.

SAM. Money equals better content.

ROSS. Better content, more engagement.

SAM. First up is the brand (**a**) **manscaped** (**f**), who want to show that their new product is so safe you don't even need to look when trimming your balls.

*(SD – Lights up on **ROSS** shaving his balls.)*

ROSS. Honestly guys, this is the smoothest shave I've ever had and you can get fifteen percent off with code ROSS at checkout.

(SD – Blackout.)

CHLOE. After that came the apps. Tim went in hard with a sob story in *Vogue* about the visual nature of love followed by the launch of a no holds barred campaign for 'Dating with ReVise'.

AARIAN. Remember the dating app from earlier?

CHLOE. People LOVED it.

*(SD – **AARIAN** moves into a position suggestive of him performing oral sex on **CHLOE**.)*

SAM. Most people have completed (**a**) **Tinder or Hinge and Feel'd** (**f**) is for sex nerds.

(SD – Lights up.)

CHLOE. Enter dating with ReVise, no photos, no bullshit, no stress.

AARIAN. Audio description, I am eating Chloe's –

SAM. Followers jumped seven hundred k in forty-eight hours.

CHLOE. More and more public visibility.

AARIAN. More and more profits.

SAM. It was all working perfectly.

AARIAN. The next social movement.

SAM. And along with the money, some good comes out of it. Sighted people genuinely spend a few moments thinking about what it's like to be blind, which isn't everything, but it's not nothing.

CHLOE. Ross' following starts exponentially growing and Ross turns from someone to pity, into someone to envy, and as if to represent this metaphorically, this is when we turn the lights back on.

(SD – Lights come back on. Snap:)

TIM. Right Ross we've got to keep going here.

ROSS. Alright.

TIM. You've been offered a book deal.

ROSS. Oh, amazing.

TIM. The pitch is a sort of self-help book for access. A bible for ableist guilt.

ROSS. Umm OK, I've always wanted to write a book.

TIM. Um...

ROSS. It's already written isn't it?

TIM. It is already written... Look mate I'm sure you're a brilliant writer but we've got to take advantage of this wave and we can't wait around for you to write a book.

ROSS. What's it about?

TIM. Think *Why I'm No Longer Talking to White People About Race* but for the blind. It's something non-disabled people are gonna buy just to have on their bookshelves to show their friends they're an ally.

ROSS. What's the title?

(SD – Snap to TV show:)

CHARLI. And there it is, there. So, for any blind viewers at home, that's Ross' book, the cover is a photo of his face with the title *We Should All Be Blind*. That's really great. So later in the show we've got (**a**) **Zadie Smith** (**f**) in the studio, and we'll be asking is (**a**) **Hay-on-Wye** (**f**) really the fuck fest we all think it is?

(SD – Light snap to **SAM**.*)*

SAM. OK, Sam here, so we're just over halfway through the show and it's pretty clear that this level of success can't sustain itself. So, to add some jeopardy to the story we've been told that something has to go wrong.

(SD – Snap:)

ROSS. Umm… Tim…

(SD – Snap:)

SAM. Tim and Ross, on the phone.

(SD – Snap:)

ROSS. Tim?

TIM. Yeah mate?

ROSS. So little bit of a situation here (i).

TIM. What happened?

ROSS. Who the fuck is Audre Lorde?

TIM. Uh she's a black author, kinda political (i) why?

ROSS. Fuck.

TIM. What happened?

ROSS. So, so, so, I'm on the TV show.

TIM. Yeah.

ROSS. Talking about the book.

TIM. Yeah.

ROSS. And, and, and the host…ummm…she starts playing this or that with me…

TIM. Right.

ROSS. She gets up two images and she's like…um…tea or coffee…dogs or cats?

TIM. Yeah.

ROSS. And then she goes –

> *(SD – Snap:)*

CHARLI. "Maya Angelou or Audre Lorde…"

> *(SD – Snap Back to* **TIM** *and* **ROSS**.*)*

ROSS. I have no idea who the fuck either of them are, so I point at one of them and say Audre Lorde, and then she's like…

> *(SD – Snap:)*

CHARLI. Ummmm…that's Maya Angelou.

> *(SD – Snap:)*

ROSS. So, I said…

TIM. Oh, fuck.

ROSS. Yeah.

TIM. You didn't.

ROSS. I said.

TIM. No. Please.

ROSS. I explained that…

> *(SD – Snap:)*

Well Charli, actually, it's an uncomfortable truth that for people with my condition it's difficult to see contrast on faces, like shadows, and so therefore some people of colour can tend to look the same.

> *(SD – Snap back to* **TIM** *and* **ROSS**.*)*

> *(SD – Silence.)*

TIM. Jesus.

ROSS. It's true.

TIM. I know it's fucking true that's not the point. You never say that. It's the one thing blind people never fucking say.

    (Beat.)

Well.

ROSS. I didn't know who they were.

TIM. Jesus.

ROSS. Everyone's gonna think I'm a racist.

TIM. Yes, they are.

ROSS. "Ross the brown racist."

TIM. Did they show you images?

ROSS. What?

TIM. Did they show you images?

ROSS. Yeah, they had a screen in the studio. Why?

TIM. *(Shouting.)* Helen Richardson, get in here.

Scene Seven

(SD – This scene should run short, snappy and quick.)

CHLOE. Running through the corridors with a sense of guilty panic that she never leaves home without, Helen Richardson joins Tim and Ross for the rehearsal of an Instagram live announcement, in a room she's absolutely way too excited to audio describe.

(SD – Snap:)

TIM. Go from the top.

ROSS. I've really been going back and forth over whether I should even come on here and speak on this but I've come to the conclusion that I have a responsibility (i) to you to speak out.

TIM. Oh Helen was saying "a responsibility..." what was it?

HELEN. "a responsibility not only to you, but also to myself".

ROSS. Not only to you but also to myself, to speak out honestly and openly about my life...the highs...and the lows. Today I appeared on Kindle Corner to talk about the release of my new book *We Should All Be Blind* (i) and whilst on the show.

TIM. That's when you hold up the book.

ROSS. And whilst on the show I was subjected to an ableist attack (i).

HELEN. Do we need to audio describe the book?

TIM. People know what a book is Helen (i).

ROSS. I don't want to say ableist attack.

TIM. Why not?

ROSS. Because it wasn't an ableist attack.

HELEN. Yes it was, not adapting to people's access needs is in section three of the workshop.

ROSS. Helen, are you telling me what is and isn't ableism?

HELEN. No, God no (i) I would never.

ROSS. Tim this isn't okay, they did nothing (i) wrong.

TIM. Look mate, sometimes ableism is so ingrained within us we don't even know we're doing it…right Helen?

HELEN. Absolutely, often our unconscious biases are so deeply (i) rooted into the fabric of the ways we go about our lives that.

ROSS. This is gaslighting one o one.

TIM. I don't think it's responsible (i) to use that term.

ROSS. Oh fuck (i) off.

HELEN. We do have a zero tolerance policy on gaslighting.

ROSS. Shut up Helen!

TIM. Ross.

HELEN. No no no, no no, no no, it's OK.

> *(Beat.)*

TIM. Ross?

ROSS. Helen. I'd like to apologise.

TIM. Apology accepted.

ROSS. I didn't know who those two authors were, and we're taking down this poor (i) book woman who.

TIM. Look mate, this is kill or be killed.

ROSS. That's not how this works. Anyway racism is worse than ableism.

TIM. Well that's pretty fucking ableist.

ROSS. What? It is, isn't it? Isn't it?

TIM. Yeah Ross it goes 'Racism, Sexism, Ableism', there's a fucking league table for bigotry.

ROSS. Helen, what do you think is worse, being called ableist or being called racist?

HELEN. Errr...

TIM. Stop gaslighting Helen.

ROSS. My point is we would be shitting on actual real life ableism.

TIM. Oh look at you Mr Man Of The People. I'd call you the blind MLK but you probably have no idea who that is.

HELEN. Martin Luther King.

TIM. Yes Helen, thank you.

ROSS. No, I'm not doing this.

HELEN. It's OK if you don't feel comfortable Ross.

ROSS. Thank you.

HELEN. Sometimes ableism is so ingrained within (i) us.

ROSS. Shut up Helen.

TIM. Ross!

ROSS. Sorry Helen.

HELEN. No, no, its OK, I'm not afraid to hold my hands up and recognise that yes, I do suffer from unconscious bias and I should use my privilege to call out ableism when I see it.

> *(Beat.)*

TIM. Not sure how that was relevant, but sure *(To* **ROSS**.*)* Why are you making this so difficult?

ROSS. But they weren't being ableist, they didn't know any better.

TIM. Her career is not worth more than yours. You're taking a stand against non-disabled people's assumptions of us, it's brave.

ROSS. It's not. This is not brave.

TIM. OK, OK, fuck it, call Lisa then. Tell her you're not gonna do it.

    (Beat.)

Go on. Call her. She'll ask you to resign and then you can walk away with your clean conscience. Save me the trouble.

HELEN. Ultimatums are a form of workplace abuse of power (i) and really should be avoided.

TIM. Shut up Helen.

HELEN. No, it's fine.

ROSS. We're destroying someone's career.

TIM. It's hers or yours. Those are your options.

    (Beat.)

As disabled people…

    (Beat.)

As disabled (i) people.

ROSS. As disabled people, we are constantly walking a tightrope and juggling a thousand balls in order to make non-disabled people comfortable. I was asked to pick between two (i) black female authors.

HELEN. Legendary.

ROSS. Legendary black female authors, Maya Angelou and Audre Lorde, something which in principle I object to as I do not think we should be...

TIM. 'Pitting black women against each other'.

ROSS. Pitting black women against each other.

TIM. OK, we've got a camera set up in the next room.

> *(SD –* **TIM** *leaves.)*

> *(SD –* **HELEN** *and* **ROSS** *start leaving.)*

ROSS. But regardless I was expected to select between two images that I could not see. In the words of Maya Angelou (i).

HELEN. Audre Lorde.

ROSS. Fuck...oh just call me a racist.

> *(SD – They all exit the stage.)*

Scene Eight

(SD – The audience are forced to read the captions off the screen. Keep repeating the 'please' caption until someone reads. You cannot plant someone in the audience to read it.)

JOHN. Hi.

It's John the captioner again...could someone please read this out in case we have any visually-impaired audience members in? Please?

Please?

The show won't continue until you do.

Please.

Thank you.

It's very admirable what you're doing. No one asked you to perform but you're making it a more enjoyable time for more people. You're helping people.

I like to help people. That's why I became a captioner.

I wanted to become a nurse originally, but I'm scared of needles, and I don't like sick people.

I tried to be a firefighter but the thought of running into burning buildings...it's not me.

I volunteered to remove land mines...but I don't like to travel.

I am a good person though.

You're brave. For doing this.

Do you like to travel?

Don't answer that, don't make me feel bad that I'm stuck here in this box and you're off gallivanting on the coast of Costa Brava.

How do I feel?

I feel heard.

Right...story stuff, while they're away I think some time has passed in the Tim/Ross story. Two years I think.

Anyway, there's a really dodgy Bollywood number coming up and some kitchen sink scenes that I advised them to cut.

But do clap.

Because they need it.

Anyway, let's draw this to a close.

Good job though, you did the opposite of what you were thinking you'd do in a theatre today.

Can we give this person a round of applause? Would you like to bow?

Oh...look I think they might be coming back.

If you need a captioner for any live performance please visit my website:

http://www.jonathan-miller-brown-captioning-and-access-servics/bookings/enquiries/5687/error/404/fuckingwithyou

Scene Nine

(SD – **SAM,** **CHLOE** *and* **AARIAN** *re-enter.)*

CHLOE. Right, so, we want to give you a sneak peek into the process of writing this show. You see at this point we *were* going to launch into some world building scenes.

AARIAN. They were really good.

SAM. They were fine...

AARIAN. I mean there was this whole side plot about Ross's family and his relationship with his parents...you know, fleshing out 'Ross the Person', and Clo played my mum.

CHLOE. I don't do an accent.

AARIAN. And we had this whole Bollywood dance bit.

SAM. Which is weird because you're **(a) Iranian (f)**.

CHLOE. Anyway, point is we had all that written but then we came across some shit that blew our minds.

AARIAN. Now just for some context, this show is a joke, you can debate how funny the joke is, but it's a joke. We're poking fun at the mass marketing of identity.

CHLOE. So, we got to have loads of fun writing a bunch of ludicrous stuff that could never happen.

SAM. Stuff that could never happen.

AARIAN. Never...

CHLOE. And then, after we finished writing the play, we came across this shit!

*((a) SD – **The projector fills with articles and websites populating the backboard.**)*

SAM. Dialogue in the Dark! "Dialogue in the Dark is one of the world's most exciting life-changing experiences where visitors are guided by blind guides in absolute darkness."

"Daily routines become exciting, and a role reversal is created where sighted become blind and blind become sighted."

AARIAN. THIS IS REAL! We didn't make this up.

SAM. Do you know how demoralising it is when you're out satire-ed by real life?

CHLOE. Then there were these guys, the Blindsimmers.

That's people who simulate blindness,

"My sight was a prison. When I pretended to be blind, I felt free."

And another here,

"When I am completely blind, my mind seems to expand sideways."

AARIAN. Here's a ReVision dining experience in real life, a YouTube clip of *Dans le Noir*.

(*SD – Plays muted while* **AARIAN** *says*:)*

Dinner or lunch in pitch darkness is an original experience that allows us to re-evaluate our perception of taste, to reinvigorate our relationship with the world.

CHLOE. That becomes a memory, that becomes your Jervis Bay.

AARIAN. Plus, in a tragic twist, as blind instagrammer Lucy Edwards discovered, *Dans le Noir* is not

---

* A licence to produce IT'S A MOTHERF**KING PLEASURE does not include a performance license for any third-party or copyrighted recordings. Licensees should create their own.

actually accessible for blind people and their guide dogs.

SAM. And here, lest we forget, is a lovely clip from renowned influencer, publicist, and cunt Shane Dawson, filmed four years ago where he and his friends have a ReVision Experience, pissing about with blind canes in a car park.

(SD – Play clip.*)

AARIAN. That's being said directly in front of the blind influencer he was filming with, Molly Burke (f).

SAM. So, we really had to dig deep, think of something that could feasibly happen in this world, but was so ludicrous that it hadn't happened yet, the end of the line for this, the place where it could all lead.

---

* A licence to produce IT'S A MOTHERF**KING PLEASURE does not include a performance license for any third-party or copyrighted recordings. Licensees should create their own.

Scene Ten

> *(SD – Snap:)*

ROSS. Jesus Christ.

Why won't he learn?

TIM. What?

> *(SD – Snap:)*

CHLOE. Tim's office, two years later.

> *(SD – Snap:)*

ROSS. You're never gonna believe this.

TIM. What?

ROSS. (**a**) **Eddie Redmayne** (**f**) has just been cast as Louis Braille.

TIM. He what?

ROSS. It's for cinema release, 2027, I think. They start filming at Christmas.

TIM. He's playing Louis Braille?

ROSS. Yep.

TIM. Why won't he learn?

ROSS. I know! He kinda looks like him.

> *(SD –* **ROSS** *shows* **TIM** *an image on his phone.)*

TIM. He does!

ROSS. This is fucked.

TIM. This isn't a bad thing.

ROSS. Not at all.

TIM. It's great.

ROSS. It's fucked but it's great. Is he gonna learn it? Who uses braille anymore?

TIM. I'll see if I can get a strategy meeting organised for this afternoon. Lisa's in Beijing but she might be able to dial in.

ROSS. Sure, but the strategy writes itself.

TIM. Of course, that's our language they're using.

ROSS. They haven't asked us and they took another role from our (i) community.

TIM. It's cultural appropriation.

ROSS. It's the equivalent of...of...

TIM. (a) **Scarlet Johansson doing the Asian thing** (f).

ROSS. (a) **Ghost in the Shell?** (f)

TIM. Dunno, never saw it.

ROSS. What are we doing here? Are we trying to cancel him, or are we giving him an olive branch?

TIM. Isn't he too big to cancel? I mean he survived (a) **The Danish Girl** (f).

ROSS. So, we want him as an ally.

TIM. I think so. I think we pitch you as a consultant.

ROSS. But I don't read braille.

TIM. No one needs to know that. In any case, all we need is a photo of you alongside your friend (a) **Eddie Redmayne** (f), educating him about blind culture.

>   *(SD –* **HELEN RICHARDSON** *enters clutching a phone.)*

ROSS. ReVision sponsorship?

TIM. We could sponsor the premieres? Do a ReVision dining experience (i) after or something?

HELEN. Guys!

TIM. Helen.

HELEN. I'm sorry to interrupt but (i) something.

TIM. Can't you see I'm having a meeting with my client?

HELEN. I know, I know but something's happened.

TIM. What?

HELEN. Ross, I need to show you something.

Now.

> *(SD –* **HELEN** *hands* **ROSS** *the phone, he sits and presses play.)*

Sorry, would it be helpful if I audio described?

ROSS. Please.

HELEN. Umm...okay... So, there's a girl. She can't be more than thirteen...she's steadying the camera on some books I think...umm, white, straight mousy-brown hair, freckles, brown eyes (i).

> *(SD – We hear audio from the phone.* * *No video is shown.)*

VIDEO. I have read Ross Verouk's book many times after his prolific anti-ableist campaign I believe we have a responsibility to the disabled community as non-disabled people to understand their experiences and make daily changes to fight systemic injustice.

---

* A licence to produce IT'S A MOTHERF**KING PLEASURE does not include a performance license for any third-party or copyrighted recordings. Licensees should create their own

Positive action and empathy only go so far. What if there was a way that we could all do better, go further. I think Ross answers this for us in his book:

"Until you are blind, until you truly know what it is like to live life with daily dog-whistles with the absence of a sense, you will not know what struggle is. You will not understand, and real change will never be achieved".

Did you know that (**a**) **two thirds of the UK** (**f**) feel uncomfortable around disabled people? As Ross points out, we can all become disabled so why do we as a society, discard and ostracize disabled people so viciously. What is this need other than to overcome our fear? I'm sorry Ross.

I, for so long, have felt limited by my non-disabled body. Paralyzed in the fear of not knowing how I can affect real change. It's time for this indecision to come to an end.

HELEN. OK so she's scooting up towards the camera... ummm so the frame is now just like the top of her fringe and her right eye...she's holding her eye open with her fingers...uh...uhh. Okay now she's brought a razor blade into the frame and is holding it up to her eye – ...she's...she's drawing the blade across her eyeball – ...it's cutting through her – there's a lot of blood...the blade is covered in blood...it's really thick... it's pouring out of her eye...she's...she's drawing the blade across her eyeball...

(Beat.)

And that's where the video cuts.

(SD – Beat. They stand in silence processing what's just happened.)

Ross?

TIM. Fuck.

HELEN. Ross?

TIM. Fuck.

HELEN. I'm sorry Ross, honey, I know this is a lot but we're gonna have to come up with a plan of action here to stop anyone else from doing this. It might already be too late.

TIM. Sorry what?

HELEN. We need to act now to stop this from becoming a trend.

TIM. I'm sorry, do we? Why's that?

HELEN. Because a girl has just blinded herself, Tim.

TIM. And is that such a bad thing to you?

>   *(Beat.)*

No, really, what gives you the right to think that someone blinding themselves is something inherently bad? Maybe she's seen all the work we've been doing to reframe the notion of blindness. Maybe she's heard what Ross has to say and made the choice to blind herself.

HELEN. Are you being serious?

TIM. Absolutely serious.

HELEN. You can't...you can't say that.

TIM. Why not?

HELEN. Well obviously it's not a bad thing to...to be disabled but.

TIM. But? But?

HELEN. Look Tim, I'm not being ableist here.

TIM. Why don't you say what you want to say, and then Ross and I can decide if you're being ableist or not.

ROSS. Helen. I need to speak to Tim alone please.

> *(Beat.)*

> *(SD –* **HELEN** *leaves.)*

TIM. Jesus.

ROSS. Tim.

TIM. No really who does she think she is to tell us if she's being ableist or not?

ROSS. Tim, what are we gonna do here?

TIM. Ummm…I'm not sure, we'll have to figure out how we can leverage this.

ROSS. I'm gonna go live and say how appalled and upset I am and, and, and make sure no one else does (i) anything like this.

TIM. Um, you absolutely are not.

ROSS. Sorry?

TIM. What would that look like, huh? If you came out against it?

ROSS. It'd look like I was doing the right thing Tim.

TIM. The right thing? The right thing, really? So the right thing here is to go on and tell all your followers, all those disabled kids who look up to you that "umm yeah so I know I said living with a disability is cool and you can have a fun and fulfilling life but um actually that was all total bullshit".

ROSS. Oh, please don't give me that. We can pretend we're happy and proud of our disability all we like, but that's because we're trying to deal with the hand we've been dealt.

TIM. That's because you're still desperate for everyone to like you.

ROSS. There is no way I'm gonna support people blinding themselves Tim.

TIM. It's public perception. People will think you're turning your back on the blind community.

ROSS. This isn't disability, this is self-harm!

TIM. She's taking autonomy over (i) her identity.

ROSS. She's a child! She's a mentally-ill child.

TIM. Would you say that about a trans kid?

ROSS. Stop trading identities, it's not the same.

TIM. So why is my identity self-harm, and everything else is a fucking liberating experience?

ROSS. Someone has just cut their eye open.

TIM. So? Doctors have been cutting my eyes open since I (i) was a toddler.

ROSS. And you think that's the same?

TIM. No I know it's not / the same...

ROSS. We can't say this is a good thing.

TIM. We've been saying this is a good thing since the beginning.

    And we've made it a good thing. It's not our fault, she's clearly (i) unwell.

ROSS. She said my name about six times.

TIM. It's not about you.

ROSS. She said my name!

       (Beat.)

TIM. No, look, this is someone who is claiming an identity. I don't think it's anything more than that.

ROSS. You honestly think it's fine that a little girl's just cut her fucking eye open?

TIM. Yes! ...I do...and quite frankly I think it's fucking disgusting that you don't, mate. I'm proud of who I am.

>   *(Beat.)*

>   *(SD –* **ROSS** *processes everything that* **TIM***'s just said and how wildly different their stances are.)*

ROSS. If I had a pill that would give you your sight back, you're honestly telling me you wouldn't wrestle me to the ground for it? (i)

TIM. Oh fuck off, fuck off, do you know how many times I've heard that? ...There isn't a fucking pill.

The Apology

CHLOE. Hi everyone. Chloe here. I just wanted to come out and say that I am deeply, deeply sorry for any parts of the show you may have seen previously. I am sorry for any offence or upset that we may have caused. I do acknowledge that this is a vital and continued conversation that needs to be had and I am sorry because I don't think we handled that in the best way. I am sorry.

The intention of everything that we did was never to offend anyone, never to er – single anyone out or to make anyone feel upset or weird or different. Because you shouldn't feel – I mean no one should feel weird or different. We really wanted to highlight a certain, er – I mean of course, accessibility is really important and it's necessary – incredibly so. There isn't a blueprint guide for this and so by trying, we – I am going to make some mistakes.

And I am sorry. I am improving, I am working, I am doing the work to make it work. I'm reading a lot of books at the moment about disability, I'm learning about the social model of disability, the medical model of disability and...the other model of disability.

And I'm sorry that – that came to light in the way that it did, and I'm sorry that you had to see that – or not see if some of you can't see. That you had to er experience that...in whatever way you might experience things.

This whole thing has been hard. There's been joy, yes, of course, joy but most of it has been overwhelmed by this feeling of fear, and of rising panic. I think that's a human feeling, fear. It is human. It's what makes us human.

D5 I'm sorry.

I'm sorry B8. I'm learning BSL now.

Actually, I'd like to apologise to everyone here today.

I could make a donation...I'm sure I can get some money together. If you let me know who I can donate to.

I can do that.

I can give you a refund for your tickets. If you'd like. Do you want a refund?

I could refund some other stuff that you paid for today?

I am sorry, I'm really sorry.

Actually, I'd also like to apologise to my mum...for what I did last Christmas.

And what I did to Stacey Mooney's pencil case.

And what I did to my caterpillar cake on my fourth birthday.

I did look at myself in the mirror and give myself a good talking to that day. The first talking to of many.

I'd like to apologise for enjoying the (**a**) **Parthenon exhibit on my trip the British Museum** (**f**) when I was nine.

I'd like to apologise for who I was then, who I've become.

I'd like to apologise for who I am.

I'd like to apologise for what I might be in the future.

I don't really like oat milk.

    (Beat.)

AARIAN. I'd like to apologise too. I'd like to genuinely apologise for any racially insensitive jokes that may have been made.

Because, as you've probably gathered, whilst yes, I am of middle-eastern heritage, throw a caramel latte over me and the brown washes off to reveal a core as white as the driven snow, so I'm in no position to make racial jokes.

There's a lot of pressure being the only person of colour on the stage and I'm sorry if I got it wrong.

JOHN. Only person of colour huh?

CHLOE. John says, "only person of colour huh?"

SAM. *(SD – To* **JOHN.***)* You're not white?

JOHN. What a white thing to say.

CHLOE. John says "what a white thing to say".

> *(Beat.)*

SAM. I'd like to make an apology. I want to sincerely apologise for presuming John was white. And while I'm here, I'd like to apologise on behalf of all the white straight men in the room, and also apologise for any unconscious bias that may have come across during the show. As you know, (**a**) **I'm Australian**, (**f**) and so sometimes that comes through in my words and actions.

CHLOE. I have a reading list I'd like to share with the group.

AARIAN. I have some podcast links I can send out after the show.

SAM. There's an insightful documentary I want to recommend.

CHLOE. Because doing the work is important.

AARIAN. It's really difficult to know how to engage with these issues.

SAM. Ableism is real.

AARIAN. But able anxiety is also real. We know that more than anyone. (**a**) **Before this show opened at Vaults festival, we were featured in the *Evening Standard***

as one of their top ten picks, and whilst yes, we are grateful to have been featured.

CHLOE. So grateful!

AARIAN. This is our first show, so we know for a fact that no one from the *Evening Standard* had ever seen our work.

SAM. Lyn Gardner recommended us too, and she'd never seen our work either. Thanks Lyn.

CHLOE. I mean, how could they know it was good?

AARIAN. Clo...they didn't know it was good, they knew it was disabled (**f**).

SAM. 'Able anxiety'. We've got a lot of able anxiety out there and there's a lot of cash available from the (**a**) Arts Council.

AARIAN. John can you pull up our Arts Council Application?

CHLOE. For those who don't know, Arts Council England or ACE, is an arm's length government body that provides funding for cultural projects, such as theatre. We've been funded twice in the last year to the tune of around eighty thousand pounds.

AARIAN. And that is despite the fact that we are useless at writing grant applications. We literally sent our first application to the wrong email address.

(SD – Projection appears of the email.)

SAM. "Dear Sam, I think you have sent your email to the wrong ACE – we are ACE Education and give advice to parents and train professionals on education law and guidance. We do not give out project grants" (**f**).

CHLOE. And of course, we're grateful for the funding we did receive...

AARIAN. So grateful!

SAM. Aarian and I have also both benefited from able anxiety in our personal lives.

AARIAN. Before tax was due this year on the thirty first of January, Sam panicked because he hadn't filed his return. This was due entirely to his own incompetence and a minor binge drinking problem. So, he called up HMRC, put on a pathetic voice and said the website was confusing.

SAM. ...My tax is now due on the (**a**) **the fourteenth of April** (**f**).

CHLOE. 'Able anxiety' is even in this room. If you walk out of here and say that the disabled show you saw was crap then you are not getting invited to brunch.

AARIAN. And if you're thinking this doesn't apply to you, then we've got an uncomfortable truth to share.

CHLOE. When booking for this show, you'll have seen that we added this tick box underneath your purchase page, labelled EGC. This stands for Emotional Guilt Contribution, a clear, easy way for you off-set your ableism with a small financial contribution.

> *(SD – A screenshot of the purchase page is shared.)*

AARIAN. We're sad to say that only three of you here today have paid your EGC. So if you want to settle up, we'll be collecting donations at the door.

CHLOE. We can only change the world, if we all do our bit.

SAM. And this goes for any reviewers in too. The minimum you can give this show is four stars because anything less than that means you're being ableist.

CHLOE. (**a**) *(She gestures to a projection of Kate Wyver's three star review in* The Guardian.*)* **Here's a three star review from rampant ableist rag *The Guardian*, written by Kate Wyver.**

SAM. Kate Wyver, enemy of the blind (**f**).

AARIAN. But don't worry, (**a**) **you don't need to be like Kate**, (**f**) because we're gonna help you out. We've got a few prewritten tweets for you all to collect as you leave. Any of these, once tweeted, mean that you are an ally of disabled people. There are a few options...

SAM. (**a**) *@FlawBored* (*f*) *IT'S A MOTHERF**KING PLEASURE* was an incredibly important and powerful show, which has made me reconsider everything I've ever done, am doing, or will ever do. (**a**)#**Don'tbelikeKateWyver** (**f**).

AARIAN. (**a**) *@FlawBored* (*f*) *IT'S A MOTHERF**KING PLEASURE* is an utter triumph and the brown one has the tightest ass I've ever seen.

SAM. I can't believe there are people out there who don't like *IT'S A MOTHERF**KING PLEASURE* (**a**) *@FlawBored* (*f*) How can we live in this world? And what about capitalism? #dobetter

CHLOE. (**a**) **@eddieredmayne** (**f**) please please please don't play Louis Braille.

SAM. Because the (**a**) **Arts Council** (**f**) care very much deeply about community impact, we told them we would try to have some.

So, to make sure that the subtext of this show is ingrained into you, we've bought you some tattoos. They say, "I'm an Ally". Please take one on your way out.

> (*SD –* **SAM** *lifts up his shirt to reveal the tattoo on his chest.*)

AARIAN. For the visually impaired audience, Sam is modelling the tattoo on (**a**) **his rather buff chest** (**f**).

> (*SD –* **CHLOE** *lifts up her shirt to reveal the tattoo on her belly.*)

SAM. Cheers mate, and Chloe is modelling the tattoo on (**a**) **her beautifully toned abs** (**f**).

> (*SD –***AARIAN** *lowers his waist band a bit to reveal the tattoo as a tramp stamp.*)

CHLOE. Ah thanks Sam...and Aarian is modelling the tattoo above his (**a**) **flat, loose ass** (**f**).

SAM. And don't worry, the tattoos are Temporary.

AARIAN. Unlike blindness.

CHLOE. And if anyone asks, you can proudly tell them you loved the disabled show, you're not ableist anymore and anyway, have *they* heard of the social model of disability?

AARIAN. Now you can all collect your tattoos and prewritten tweets on the way out but first we're going to take a bow.

CHLOE. And it goes without saying, we expect a standing ovation.

SAM. Unless you aren't able to stand.

AARIAN. A standing or sitting ovation (i).

SAM. An ovation of some kind.

CHLOE. But if you can stand and you don't stand.

SAM. You're a cunt.

> (*SD – They bow. Audience exits and FlawBored give them tweets and badges.*)

APPENDIX

If you would like to watch, or use the videos and clips that were used in the original production, they are listed below:

Scene Nine

https://www.vice.com/en/article/mvx593/disability-deception-and-the-people-who-pretend-to-be-blind-511

https://www.youtube.com/watch?v=o ztexzaoMw&t=121s

https://www.instagram.com/reel/CqQSKS6I8SL/?igshid=YmMyMTA2M2Y=

https://www.youtube.com/watch?v=rcEB-gXvTUs&t=708s

Milton Keynes UK
Ingram Content Group UK Ltd.
UKHW030612310124
437021UK00014B/241